Weather Watchers

Sunshine

Cassie Mayer

www.heinemann.co.uk/library

Visit our website to find out more information about Heinemann Library books.

To order:

☎ Phone 44 (0) 1865 888066

Send a fax to 44 (0) 1865 314091

📄 Visit the Heinemann Bookshop at www.heinemann.co.uk/library to browse our
💻 catalogue and order online.

First published in Great Britain by Heinemann Library,
Halley Court, Jordan Hill, Oxford OX2 8EJ, part of Harcourt
Education. Heinemann is a registered trademark of Harcourt
Education Ltd.

Editorial: Tracey Crawford, Cassie Mayer, Dan Nunn,
and Sarah Chappelow
Design: Jo Hinton-Malivoire
Picture Research: Tracy Cummins, Tracey Engel,
and Ruth Blair
Production: Duncan Gilbert

Originated by Chroma Graphics (Overseas) Pte. Ltd
Printed and bound in China by South China
Printing Company

ISBN 978 0 431 18259 9 (hardback)
11 10 09 08 07
10 9 8 7 6 5 4 3 2 1

ISBN 978 0 431 18376 3 (paperback)
12 11 10 09 08
10 9 8 7 6 5 4 3 2 1

British Library Cataloguing in Publication Data
Mayer, Cassie
 Sunshine. - (Weather watchers)
 1.Sunshine - Juvenile literature
 I.Title
 551.5'271

Acknowledgements
The publishers would like to thank the following for permission
to reproduce photographs: Corbis pp. 4 (cloud; rain, Anthony
Redpath), 5 (G. Schuster/zefa), 7 (Royalty Free), 8 (Theo Allofs),
9 (zefa/Sergio Pitamitz), 10 (Chris Sattlberger), 11 (Royalty Free),
12 (Royalty Free), 13 (Galen Rowell), 14 (Reuters), 15 (epa/Karl-
Josef Hildenbrand), 16 (Richard Klune), 17 (zefa/S. Andreas), 18
(Royalty Free), 19 (zefa/Jason Horowitz), 20 (George D. Lepp), 21
(ROB & SAS), 23 (heat wave, Reuters; snow scene, epa/Karl-Josef
Hildenbrand); Getty Images pp. 4 (lightning; snow, Marc Wilson
Photography), 6 (Tim McGuire).

Cover photograph reproduced with permission of Corbis (Howard
Kingsnorth/zefa). Back cover photograph reproduced with
permission of Corbis (George D. Lepp).

Every effort has been made to contact copyright holders of any
material reproduced in this book. Any omissions will be rectified in
subsequent printings if notice is given to the publishers.

Contents

What is weather?

There are many types of weather.
Weather changes all the time.

A sunny day is a type of weather.

What is sunshine?

Sunshine is light from the sun.

Sunshine feels warm
on your skin.

Sunshine heats the land.

Sunshine heats the ocean.

The Sun rises in the morning.
Then it is light outside.

The Sun sets in the evening.
Then it is dark outside.

In the middle of the day the Sun is high in the sky. The sunshine is strong.

In the mornings and evenings the Sun is low in the sky. The sunshine is weak.

Sunshine and the seasons

Sunshine is strong in the summer.
Summer days can be hot.

Sunshine is weak in the winter.
Winter days can be cold.

Sunshine around the world

Countries near the equator
have strong sunshine. These
countries are warm all year.

Countries far from the equator have weak sunshine. These countries are cold all year.

Sunshine safety

Sunshine can burn your skin.
Always stay covered in the Sun.

Sunshine can hurt your eyes.
Never look right at the Sun.

How does sunshine help us?

Living things need sunshine to grow.

Sunny days can be fun!

What to wear in the sun

hat

sunglasses

sun cream

long-sleeved shirt

Picture glossary

summer the time of year
when it is warmest

winter the time of year
when it is coldest

Index

Notes to parents and teachers
Before reading
Talk about different weather. Ask the children which type of weather they like best. Talk about how the Sun is warmer in the summer than in the winter, as the Sun is closer in the summer.

After reading
Play "Sun and Rain". Select one child to be the rain and another to be the sun. The rest of the children run around within a specified area. If caught by the rain, children must stand still, arms and legs outstretched, until "released" by the Sun who crawls through their legs. Sing: "The Sun has got his hat on, Hip, Hip, Hip Hurray".
Share with the children the traditional story "The Sun and the Wind".
Sprinkle some mustard seeds on damp newspaper. Place some in a dark cupboard and the rest on a sunny windowsill. Compare how each grows. Talk about how plants need sunshine to grow.